THE POETRY TRIALS

SOUTHERN VERSES

Edited By Jenni Bannister

Years of YoungWriters

First published in Great Britain in 2016 by:

Coltsfoot Drive
Peterborough
PE2 9BF
Telephone: 01733 890066
Website: www.youngwriters.co.uk

FOREWORD

Welcome, Reader!

For Young Writers' latest competition, *The Poetry Trials*, we gave secondary school pupils nationwide the challenge of writing a poem. They were given the option of choosing a restrictive poetic technique, or to choose any poetic style of their choice. They rose to the challenge magnificently, with young writers up and down the country displaying their poetic flair.

We chose poems for publication based on style, expression, imagination and technical skill. The result is this entertaining collection full of diverse and imaginative poetry, which is also a delightful keepsake to look back on in years to come.

Here at Young Writers our aim is to encourage creativity in the next generation and to inspire a love of the written word, so it's great to get such an amazing response, with some absolutely fantastic poems.

I'd like to congratulate all the young poets in *The Poetry Trials - Southern Verses* - I hope this inspires them to continue with their creative writing.

Jenni Bannister

CONTENTS

Harris Girls' Academy East Dulwich, London

Brieya Pottinger	47
Tabitha Odutayo (14)	48

Hayle Community School, Hayle

Jessica Mills (12)	50
Grace James (11)	51
Sam Masters (12)	52
Julia Lutzka (12)	54
Ryan Harrison (12)	55
Jasmine Pearson (11)	56
Ben Pellow (12)	57
Jowan Trewartha (12)	58

John O'Gaunt School, Hungerford

Joanne Vallance (12)	59
Hannah Glover (14)	60
Katherine Natton-Bell (12)	61
Emily Allsop (13)	62

Reddam House, Wokingham

Rocio Lopez Lajo (12)	63
Max McLean (13)	64
Jack Stannah (13)	66
Harriett Howard (12)	67

Redroofs Theatre School, Maidenhead

Natasha Blaize Archer (11)	68
Lauren Murphy (12)	70

Ryde School With Upper Chine, Ryde

Katherine Bradshaw (11)	71
Aisling Nuttall (14)	72
Elsa Wester (12)	73
Sneha Sanyal (12)	74
Tilly Ashton (12)	75
Florence Tweddle (12)	76
Ben Haworth (12)	77
Jacob Swann (12)	78
Alex Wilson (12)	79
Ella Morgan Laird (12)	80
Edward Ardley (12)	81
Daisy Pink (11)	82
Thomas Luke (12)	83
Imran Rahman (11)	84
Caitlin Dingle (12)	85

Simmons House Classroom, London

Shravani Philpot (14)	86

St Leonards Academy, St Leonards-On-Sea

Jade Ball (11)	88
Millie Kemp (12)	89
Lucy Green (13)	90
Adam Elfero (12)	92
Lewis Greathead (13)	93
Chelsey Kelly (13)	94
Shakira Helsdown (14)	95

The Gryphon School, Sherborne

Sam Hinton	96

The Hope Service, Guildford

M (16)   97

Warminster School, Warminster

Maisie Craven-Smith (13)   98
Rose Elsden (13)   99
Milly Morgan (12)   100
James Burn-Leefe (13)   101
Lucy Farey (13)   102
Archie Fogg (13)   103
Ronan McKeigue (12)   104
Thea Knight (13)   105

Wilmington Academy, Dartford

Jade Louise Baldwin (13)   106
Millie Edmundson (12)   107
Bradley Alan Sapsford (12)   108
Grace Nash   109
Madison Stockburn   110
Dylan Carter Booth (13)   111
Finlay Goodger (12)   112
Ben Gifford (12)   113
Sonny George Anderson (13)   114
Kennedy Bates (12)   115
Millie Rose (13)   116
Archie Copley (11)   117
George Warner (12)   118
Louis James Childs (13)   119
Floss Goulter (12)   120
Jaden Rose   121

Winchmore School, London

Shannon Enishta   122
Mattarooa (14)
Aleyna Degirmen (12)   124

Mustafa-Berk Ak (12)   126
Klea Ndoj (12)   128

Worle Community School, Weston-Super-Mare

Leon Malins (14)   129

THE POEMS

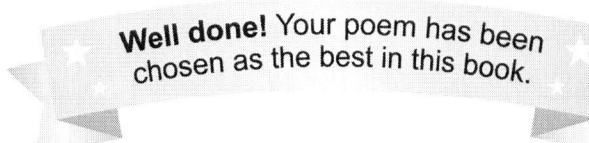

Dark Enlightenment

A thirst for knowledge, once fulfilled
Becomes a thirst for blood.
The realisation hits me,
Like a body with a thud.
The photos in the newspapers
The death next to the green.
For every peaceful village there's one bombed behind the scenes.
For every healthy child there's a starving one as well.
For every soul in Heaven there's a
Thousand more in hell.

Leon Mayne (14)
Worle Community School, Weston-Super-Mare

Broken Souls

When I was only small,
My father said he loved me,
The first time I smiled, my dad said he was proud.
The first steps I took,
Were towards my faith in books,
Where my daddy spent his time, though my mummy disallowed.

When I'd just turned nine,
My mum said she was fine,
Though her eyes were empty, and her smile was upside down.
Mum said Daddy was away,
On a little holiday,
But little did I know of how he roamed above our town.

Then Mummy started doing things,
She threw away all her rings,
And we had a bonfire fuelled by Daddy's books.
Then she started hurting me,
Leaving scars I couldn't see,
And there were bruises on my face so I got funny looks.

One day, when I missed him too much,
I put myself in Daddy's clutch,
That's why I'm here with him today, watching with the angels.
Mummy's brain is sick, you see?
When healers came she tried to flee,
But I knew doctors wouldn't help; Mum taught that from the cradle.

She said, 'Doctors are amazing,
They'll fix your bruises whole,
But though they can solve many things,
They can't fix broken souls.'

Kayleigh Muttschall (13)
Chipping Norton School, Chipping Norton

A Murder Foretold

Out in the country between two hills,
Lies a dark secret which needs to be told,
Down in the valley under the mist,
A body lies lifeless,
Untouched by love.

Her spleen is just visible, swarming with life,
As the bugs of the valley take what they need,
Something happened here,
Of which you ought to know,
What happened here to this unfortunate girl?

Entering the valley she looked all around,
Spying upon a figure lurking in the dark,
Emerging, she noticed the knife,
But she was not fast enough,
The knife plunged deep and scarlet drops scattered the ground.

Her body fell limp as jets of scarlet erupted from her throat,
She knew it was the end,
As her soul slipped away,
Leaving her body to lie there forever,
Awaiting the day for the story to be told.

Now you have been told this horrific story,
Beware! The knife that lurks in the dark,
For just before her death,
A story was told:
A girl once went to a beautiful lake,
Where a knife from the darkness,
Pierced her heart.

Zoe Allan
Chipping Norton School, Chipping Norton

The Only Answer

As I look into the glass,
I see someone else entirely,
Staring, haunting my dreams.
I know it's not right,
But it's the only answer.

At the table I feel the glare set on me,
As I push the food around my plate,
Everyone judging, almost hating me.
I know it's not right,
But it's the only answer.

As I stare into the glass once more,
I seem to be growing larger,
Even though my clothes no longer fit.
I know it's not right,
But it's the only answer.

As I walk through the town,
My eyes wander about at all the other people,
Their amazing bodies taunting me.
I know it's not right,
But it's the only answer.

As I gaze into the glass for the last time,
At the obese figure in front of me,
I can almost feel the skeleton on my shoulder,
I know it's not right,
But it's the only answer.

As I lay upon my deathbed, I think of my life
All my hopes and dreams just crushed.
I kick myself hard because
I knew it was not right.
But I thought it was the only answer.

Emily Daisy Cox (12)
Didcot Girls' School, Didcot

The World

W onderful creations
H unger and starvation
A ction and frustration
T rends are being made

I deas are changing
S tyles are creating

T echnology is progressing
H ope is belonging
E volution is happening

W hat is the world becoming?
O ld people cared for
R ights proclaimed
L ives saved
D ecisions made

B ravery
E nvironment
C ancer
O rganisation
M oney
I nnovation
N ature
G overnment

N eed
O ne
W orld

Siena Dornan Juffkins (12)
Didcot Girls' School, Didcot

6

My Mind

A mess of emotions.
An endless pit of the deepest black,
Getting lost was a huge mistake.
In the bleak dark tunnels of damp cold nothing
The smell of hate and tears filled my nostrils
I saw myself in a crumpled heap on the ground
Like a shadow of myself
My cuts were hard and concentrate like snakes
Winding up my limp arms.
My eyes were hollow and constant,
Pools of pain.
A storm grew inside of me like fire, burning on a
Fuel of misery.
I tore down the unforgiving walls of seeping vengeance
And unveiled the faithful walls of pure joy
That had waited for so long to shine through.
A patient silence, that had been waiting, waiting
For me to come home.
I was engulfed with exhilaration and it began to diffuse
Through my sore, abused body it trickled up my cold, sinister veins
And to my heart.
The very same heart that had only a whisper of a beat,
A brush of a movement.
It spread like a warm, golden butter
Into all my cracks, my discarded cuts.
My face relaxed to a smile for the first time in months.
My scars are still there, but they are fading every day.

Ellie Speakman (12)
Didcot Girls' School, Didcot

Beauty

Beauty, it's a fascinating thing,
It can be vicious,
It can be kind,
It can be angry,
It can be sublime,
Beauty covers you with a false identity
Introduces you to a whole new perspective of life itself,
Care for it, and it cares for you.
Neglect it and it will be cruel to you,
For as long as it pleases,
Everyone views beauty differently,
They see it as either a precious baby
Or an angry devil,
But you'll never know unless you try it,
And until you try it you'll never know.
If beauty likes you
It eats your flaws away like a mask
You can remove each day,
But there is another way.
Natural beauty.
It's always considerate,
It's always caring,
It's always honest,
It's always challenging.
Do you know the most fascinating thing?
Everyone has it.

Neve Isobel Lofthouse (12)
Didcot Girls' School, Didcot

Alone And Lost

My family and friends, how dreadful it is
To see them die when I'm free to live
The world is cruel but most people are kind
I stress the word 'most' and let me explain why...

There are demons and angels but how do we know
Which ones will stay and which ones will go?
Never make friends with the wrong type of guy
Or he'll learn everything about you and won't keep your hopes alive.

If you ever feel that you are alone
Nowhere to turn and no place to call home
If you have a skill for losing loved ones
Then strap in for the ride, it's not gonna be fun.

So listen up now, this is important
Everyone who's lonely has something they want
It's simple, really, and anyone can come
They just want someone to make them feel loved.

If you feel like you're lonely and just want a friend
Then don't worry, you're not alone; you'll have friends 'til the end.

Beth Eloise Reed (12)
Didcot Girls' School, Didcot

Me And My Uncle

You never said you were leaving,
You never said goodbye,
You are always in my heart,
But, I wish you were by my side.

You were always there for me,
When I needed you the most,
But, then you left me,
I was a young little girl.

But the amount that I miss you and love you,
Will always be the same,
I wish you were here today,
Every day.

But, there is a time in life when you have to go,
Up into heaven,
The brightest star in the sky.
You are amazing.

You are my uncle.

Jessica Bunce (12)
Didcot Girls' School, Didcot

Stan

I have a dog named Stanley.
He's as cute as can be.
We got him when he was eight weeks old
And now he's three.

He has more toys than Toys "R" Us,
And in the summer, his own pool.
We dress him up in hoodies and hats
And think he looks really cool.

Stan wakes up early with my dad
To get his favourite treat.
He then goes to wake my mum
And snuggle down by her feet.

He's black and white with a really fluffy tail.
He hates the postman and loves to rip up the mail.
He's terribly funny and really cheeky.
He's the smallest and craziest dog ever, but he's
Mine!

Gracie Whittington (12)
Didcot Girls' School, Didcot

I Lost My Dog Yesterday

I lost my dog yesterday.
Her name was Holly.
Oh how she loved to play.
She was a Border collie.

I lost my dog yesterday.
Thirteen years she was my friend.
With a ball, she loved to play.
I can't believe our friendship has come to an end.

I lost my dog yesterday.
We used to have Jess, her sister.
She also loved to play
And Holly really missed her.

I lost my dog yesterday.
Doggy Heaven they will attend.
Oh how they loved to play.
It will take a long time for my heart to mend.

Harriet Smith (12)
Didcot Girls' School, Didcot

Being 11

I am eleven,
Being eleven is OK,
Well, most of the time.

Because in my house,
I am the youngest,
My brother gets more.

He just turned sixteen,
My sister turned thirteen,
So she gets more.

I am nearly twelve,
I am really excited,
Only three more days!

But for now I am,
Still only eleven years old,
Boring eleven.

Tori Robinson (11)
Didcot Girls' School, Didcot

The Midnight Horse

T he Midnight Horse rode along by a
H ollow tree at midnight with
E vil round every corner lurking.

M y ears can hear her trotting
I slowly see what I came to see but
D oes this horse have a name?
N o one was able to find out
I am the only one who has seen her.
G iant trees are everywhere, this
H orse only comes out at night
T he night grew darker, this

H orse was running from an evil
O ver lakes and mountains
R unning to a safe place
S he approached me and we gazed and
E ventually I knew her name.

Caitlin Foster (12)
Didcot Girls' School, Didcot

It's Gone Now

The world is ruined,
The world is bad,
The world is deserted,
The world is sad,
I used to play games,
Out in the sun,
I used to sing songs,
With my mum,
I used to love,
I used to long,
For hopes and dreams,
For me to see,
To fall in love,
There is no one left,
To see my eyes
But they're all gone,
I'm the only one.

Lily Wakefield (12)
Didcot Girls' School, Didcot

School Life

The alarm clock whimpers, as the early hours groan.
My mum paints a smile on my face before I have to go.
The snap of the book binder says I am ready.
Oh gosh, good grief, this is a tragedy.

When I get to school, the bell says 'come in'.
The sarcastic smiles make me grin.
I open my book to find inside
What I think is a big surprise.

On a Post-it, all shiny and pink,
I can't, oh no! I need a drink.
OK, in green swirly lines
Is my overdue homework.

Ellie May (12)
Didcot Girls' School, Didcot

Time

Tick tock, tick tock
It will never stop
Never past, never future,
Always present.
Tick tock, tick tock
When will it stop?
Always changing
Never staying.
Tick tock, tick tock
Old castles to ruins
Ancient monuments to nothing.
Tick tock, tick tock
Time will never stop.
Tick tock, tick tock

Jennifer Oakley (11)
Didcot Girls' School, Didcot

Goals

Goals are what you reach for,
Even when you're tired.

Goals are what give you hope,
That you can become better.

If you don't have goals,
You can never be who you aspire.

Without goals in your life,
The pages in your life won't fit together.

Goals are important in your life,
They keep you aiming higher.

Sarra Laycock (12)
Didcot Girls' School, Didcot

The Ocean Night

The ocean, the ocean, the ocean
Glows and it shows all the creatures lurking there.
Ocean, why do you sing the song of love?
The ocean shows such great things waiting to touch my toes.
But no one knows.
The stars shine so bright wishing to touch the tide.
Ocean, why do you look so blue?
Or could it just be you?
Day after day, night after night, you glow.
I hope one day someone will see you show.
And then they will know.
How I wish for you to touch my pinkie toe.
This is the ocean, this is the ocean, this is the ocean.

Roseanna Kathleen Stoodley (12)
Didcot Girls' School, Didcot

When Everything Changes!

When everything changes
You feel lost with no home.
When everything changes
And he's not there any more.
When everything changes
You feel so small.
When everything changes
And you want the world to be no more.
When everything changes
You feel no hope and no glory.
When everything changes
And they're gone. That's my story.

Lucy Kate Maughan (12)
Didcot Girls' School, Didcot

Parents

Money-earner
Hard-worker
Job-keeper
Long-driver
Food-shopper
Argument-stopper
Meal-cooker
Child-looker
Homework-motivator
Garden-slaver
Sun cream-coverer
Family-lover!

Genevieve Carey (12)
Didcot Girls' School, Didcot

Waterdrops

Plop, plop, plop
Go raindrops
Falling down the drain
Sadness is covering the pain
Plop, plop, plop
Go teardrops
Falling on the floor
Never going to see your friends

Anna Schüder (12)
Didcot Girls' School, Didcot

Freedom

Freedom cannot be bought or sold,
It doesn't matter if you are young or old.
You'll pour your heart out to a complete stranger
Not knowing how much you put yourself in danger.
You'll look left and you'll look right,
But you know that you'll never be able to put up a fight.

Alice Hosen (12)
Didcot Girls' School, Didcot

They See Yellow

Along the beach they run,
With massive smiles on their faces.
As they enjoy the sun,
Taking big paces.
Eating their ice creams,
And dreaming big dreams.

Nisa Gharti Magar (11)
Didcot Girls' School, Didcot

The Chinese Teddy Bear!

The gentle giant lying in a forest full of bamboo,
With the risk of danger.
With its gorgeous dark brown eyes
Blending in with its soft black and white fur.
Living in the wild in the large forests of China,
Eating its medium-sized canes of bamboo.
Protected by the world's well-known charity
'The World Wildlife Fund'.
Loved, adored and cared for
By the citizens of China.
We will do all we can to protect
This endangered species.
People across the world
Who care for these large teddy bears
Do all they can to protect the wonderful species of panda.

Stacie Morris
Felpham Community College, Bognor Regis

My Dad And I

With the car packed with rod and line
For a day's fishing with Dad and I.
With dreams of clear blue open seas
And thoughts of what Mum will be cooking for our tea.
Two rods and lines were sent out to sea
With the hope that Mum will be cooking plaice for our tea.
Out there for a while, this was clearly not the place to be
As we caught no plaice for our tea.
With the car packed in a hurry
It's off to McDonald's for a Big Mac and a McFlurry.

Daniel Tidmarsh
Felpham Community College, Bognor Regis

My First Bike

Finally it was my birthday...
I was about to get a new bike,
I could feel it,
Almost touch it...

I awake, excitement coursing through me like venom,
Greeted by a stack of cards, shining banners and hugs,
The biggest package looked just like I was hoping for...
My first bike.

I asked whether I could open it,
I was answered with a nod and a sweet smile,
Instantly tearing the wrapping paper, shredding it into pieces,
A shiny red, blue and white bike was revealed,
Bearing the letters 'BMX' across it.

I took it out for a ride, but only in the never-used car park,
I climbed on the saddle and started to pedal,
Realising I was wobbling, I lost confidence and fell,
Covering my hands and knees in bits of gravel and dirt.

Helped up almost instantly by my mum, I tried again,
Many attempts later I was riding with ease,
The air whipping my face...
Occasionally doing a good swerve around a stone.

It was time to see other relatives,
Slowly I trudged into the house into the back garden...
And put the bike away...
My first bike.

Bailey Vine (11)
Felpham Community College, Bognor Regis

Seasons

In spring the sky is blue,
Leaves are green,
Flowers bloom,
In the burning sun,
The melting snow lay,
Melting more and more day by day.

After spring comes summer,
School is now over,
What a bummer,
Kids playing and having fun,
But when they see the ice cream van,
They all run.

As autumn approaches,
The leaves start to fall,
Off the trees that are very tall,
Now the temperature starts to fall,
It now does not feel like summer at all.

Finally it is now winter,
And the snow starts to fall,
Summer is like a distant memory
That never happened at all,
Children get excited as Christmas is on the way,
Hoping for enough snow for Rudolph to pull the sleigh,
Now Christmas has been and gone,
The new year starts to come,
Spring is on the way, soon to be over and done.

Chloe Cox
Felpham Community College, Bognor Regis

Teddy Bear

You never really realised,
You never really saw,
The tiny little teddy bear open up your door.

You thought you were hearing things,
You thought you were going mad,
Little did you know, this sound was of someone sad.

You stood up into your slippers,
You stood up off your bed,
To see a tiny little teddy bear turn a crimson sort of red.

'You dear little child,
Well, you see,
It's my family, they've left me!'

You picked him up,
You hugged him tight,
You held him close, throughout the night.

You loved his eyes,
You loved his nose,
You loved him from his head to toes.

And then came the goodbyes,
And then came the sorrow,
But then the bear promised he'd be back tomorrow!

Katie Croucher (12)
Felpham Community College, Bognor Regis

Birthday Memory

I woke up
On a bright, shining morning.
I looked around,
Looked at the time
And realised it was my birthday.
It was 5 o'clock in the morning
So I grabbed a book and started reading.

After two hours
I stopped reading,
Went downstairs.
There were none of the usual 'Happy Birthday' decorations,
Then I went into the living room,
That was when it began...

I jumped from the sound of 'Happy Birthday Ben',
I saw a table
And it was full of presents.
I turned ninety degrees anti-clockwise
And found my family.

I opened all my presents,
Each one gave forth a surprise
But the best of all...
Had to be my new iPhone.

Benjamin Mackley
Felpham Community College, Bognor Regis

My Memory Of Australia

At 6am we woke up dreading the flight,
Getting all our packing in the car was very tight,
Off we went on our way to the airport,
Extremely excited for our holiday ahead,
We made it through security without any problems,
The next thing we knew they were calling for our flight,
17 hours on the plane was a real pain,
Watching lots of films and playing lots of games,
Finally we were there, we made it to Oz,
Collecting our bags and hiring a car,
Meeting my cousins for the first time in four years,
Off we went to their great big house,
Extremely excited to see what it was like,
Hoping there was a swimming pool as it was so hot,
30 minutes later we arrived at the house,
Unpacking all our clothes and tidied them all away,
The next thing I knew we were playing in their swimming pool,
On a day out I heard my sister shout, 'Ooh! There is a kangaroo!'
We went to the park, it was lush and green
With lots of people enjoying the scene,
Free barbecue for one and all,
There was no charge, which was very cool.
A week before we left my nan flew out as well,
I love being with my family in the sun, having fun.

Jak Charles Allen (12)
Folpham Community College, Bognor Regis

Peace Bird, Peace

The beautiful bird's body is silky snow,
Its wings glide up and down,
In its path peace is left behind,
Wars cease,
Caged animals are freed to go to the wild,
Anger is brushed away like a fly,
Wherever the peace bird goes peace will follow.

Peace birds live in olive trees,
Because they are a sign of new life,
Or were,
Once
Upon
A time.
Without the peace birds there would be no peace
And wars would never ever cease,
Caged animals would never be freed,
Or lead the life they're meant to lead,
We know of peace birds because of one thing,
Their snow-white feathers cascade randomly,
Wherever they go.
And they are known as the peace bird's peace.

Francesca Louise Nelmes (12)
Felpham Community College, Bognor Regis

Love

Round and round we go,
Singing our song high and low.
Our song of love,
Our song of life.

We choose what we want to hear.
Love's a summer song and cheer
And a winter's headache.

Life is ours,
We sing what we like.
Come sun or sprinkling showers,
Through day and night.
No matter what the hour.

We can give a tune to everything,
Sing our song
To our heart's content.
Of love's ballad and death's lament.

Our song is here to be heard.

Megan Tanswell (13)
Felpham Community College, Bognor Regis

Animal Poem

Snakes slither
And cats sleep
Birds fly
And horses leap!

Dogs bark
And bunnies bounce
Guinea pigs squeak
And predators pounce!

Tigers roar
And deer dash
Pigs snort
And mice squeak!

All of the above
Are kind and sweet
If you're good
You might get one as a birthday treat!

Courtney Caterina, Ellen Clarke (11)
Felpham Community College, Bognor Regis

My Degu's Life In Her Cage

Her bushy tail is curled up,
Her feet pound on the wood shavings,
She climbs onto her wheel
And goes round it like a car wheel!

And when she jumps off her wheel,
Her food bowl sits in front of her.
She holds the food with her hands
And munches until it is all gone.

But when her sister comes along,
She squeaks, causing her to run.
Now she is in a corner watching her sister,
Thoughts pack inside her head,
'Now you know my life in a cage.
I want to be a human,
Free from captivity and people,' she says.

Christina Victoria Pollington (11)
Felpham Community College, Bognor Regis

Silver Sunlight

As I stood on the hill
The sunset sank down
Shining like lightning
As the moon crept up behind me
Casting a silver light, outlining the forest to my right.
I held the toy close to my chest,
And looked at the place that I never wanted to leave,
But I heard a voice calling my name,
I pulled the coat around me and tried to block the sound
But it was slowly getting louder, draining the bird song
The hill started to blur, like chalk in the rain.
It all turned white as I blinked. Once. Twice.
As my room came into focus
'Did you have a good sleep?'
'Yes. I went there again.'

Emily Holyoake (12)
Felpham Community College, Bognor Regis

The Mysterious Place

I turn up at a cosy place,
Filled with excitement and joy,
People with their families and friends,
The smell of alcohol and cigarettes roam the air,
So the doors open, carrying a breeze of fresh air,
Clearing the air of toxicity,
I go outside into the fresh warm air,
With the sun beaming down onto me,
We travel down a cliff with trees and stones,
We arrive at a mysterious place filled with families,
Looking at these wooden pieces of art,
I walk away from this tree-covered place
Through the calming green trees,
I slowly close my eyes
Into a peaceful world of imagination.

Jack Smith (12)
Felpham Community College, Bognor Regis

Memory Of Summer Fun

Early morning birdsong stirs me from my slumber,
The sun streams through the shutters like shards of golden glass.
I am enticed to open my sleepy eyelids,
I hear waves gently lapping against the rocks in the harbour.
A day at the beach beckons me.
On my way I pass white-washed buildings;
Closely packed to shade the well-worn flagstones,
I pass lazy cats, warming their tummies on sunbaked rooftops,
I finally pass by fishermen in their brightly-coloured boats,
Before me I see the glistening, clear sea,
I see tiny fish glinting as they dart through the water,
I feel my feet sinking in warm sand.
I dip my toe into the sea and...
Shiver!

Matthew Wilkinson
Felpham Community College, Bognor Regis

The Fact That

The fact that they're suffering
The fact that they're in pain
The fact that they're going to leave
And leave to a special place
The fact that you won't see them ever again
The fact that you can't share special moments in your life with them
The fact that you have to get over it
But never actually will...
The fact that there will be a point in life
That you'll be put in the exact same spot as them
In pain and dying,
No hope or anything,
Just looking into the darkness
And closing your eyes and never waking up ever again.

Katie Sarah Ferris (12)
Felpham Community College, Bognor Regis

To Be Me

To be me,
I love to go out with the dogs,
I love to play archery,
I love to play on the Xbox as well.

I like to read comics
And horror books as well,
I like to go to the beach,
I also like to go out with friends.

I don't really like going to school
But sometimes it's a good day,
It's OK to be me
Because it's always a good day.

Ethan Short (12)
Felpham Community College, Bognor Regis

My Animal Poem

Brightly-coloured beaks and silky soft black and white feathers
Soaring across the frozen sky as fast as the wind
Diving under the enormous crashing waves,
powerfully swimming for our lunch
Tiny wriggling eels desperately trying to escape from our grasp

Steep, craggy cliffs as tall as mountains are our home,
they keep us safe and warm
Our futures are born in a cosy burrow and grow big and strong
A watchful eye is cautiously looking out for danger above
A sneaky predator is hunting us down,
ready to swoop like a fighter jet
We return to the icy ocean, to continue our quest.

Nicky Joe Good (12)
Felpham Community College, Bognor Regis

Not So Goodwood

One Bank Holiday
I went to Goodwood,
Betting on the horses as you would.
My brother and I went off to the park,
Expecting good things,
But it was a shame because it was a bit lame.
While I was climbing a ladder I fell off, hitting my head,
And scared my brother who thought I was dead.
He ran off to get my mum who got help,
And I was taken away and they glued up my scalp.

Eddie Williams (12)
Felpham Community College, Bognor Regis

Comic Books

C aptain Cold is ready with his cold gun

O ld or young, how old do you think Wolverine is?

M agneto leading the mutant brotherhood

I n every one of us there is a superhero

C ool for all readers

S pider-Man says, 'With great power comes great responsibility.'

Archie Strowger (12)
Felpham Community College, Bognor Regis

Stay The Night

As I stare at your smile,
I feel the warmth of your body next to mine.
Cuddling close together,
In the cooling weather.

I don't want this to end,
But it seems like I'm on the edge.

Your smile turned to cries,
While you took off your disguise.
I'm holding onto the past,
Although it has already passed.

'Stay the night,' I cry.
To me you were the perfect guy.
I'm about to fall apart,
In my eyes, you're a beautiful piece of art.

Juan Poggioli
Full Circle Education, London

Being A Teenager In Today's Society

All of these gangs,
Young people dying,
I just want to see the world
And not my mum crying.

I'm trying to get good grades,
Keep my head up in school,
I had to change my ways,
Same time I've got to stay cool.

Twitter, 'Insta' and Snapchat,
Like a diary of a kid's life;
Nike, Airmax and a snapback,
Are just teen stereotypes.
I can't make you stay away from the knives,
But trust me;
My advice could save your life.

Jordan Spencer
Full Circle Education, London

Teen Life

I am just a young teenage girl
Just trying not to fail,
Constantly trying to do well
But nobody can tell,
If I carry on with this state of mind
The only place I will make it is jail.
Everyone's always saying it's not about anyone else,
They say just be yourself!
But it's hard when I'm just a young teenage girl,
Stereotyped, jealous and judged.
Jaded from the world,
Will I make it in this world or am I fading from the world?

Billie-Jo Marquiss
Full Circle Education, London

Before She Comes Home

Drip,
Drip,
Drip,
A leak in the tap.
My fingers are shrivelled like prunes,
Getting the sink cleared up

Before she comes home.

The thick smoke suffocates my lungs,
The bitter smell of burnt skin lingers in the room,
Panicked pacing up and down,
Preparing dinner

Before she comes home.

Scrubbing the floor till I notice my reflection,
Heaving bursts of fog onto the window,
Beads of sweat crawl down my forehead,
House polished up

Before she comes home.

Scurrying up to the bedroom,
Showering myself in a cloud of white powder,
Smothering my lips with rouge red liquid,
Knock. Knock. Knock.

She's home.
She looks in the sink, she looks at the dinner,
She looks at me

And locks the door.

Brieya Pottinger
Harris Girls' Academy East Dulwich, London

You Wish

You wish
You wish you were perfect.
Hips too wide, curves won't hide,
lean more to one side,
mind the fact it's in your mind.
Anorexic.
Broken glass.

Why don't you stick to the pages of the magazine, girl?
Cut them out like you cut your skin - tenfold,
repeat, double, unfold, don't clean.
Rip it out, stick it, rip it out, stick it, rip it out.

Who's the real you, girl?
You're just another doll, on the highest shelf.
Look at you.
'I want the one with the marble eyes.'
'No, she's not right, she's not perfect.'

What are you, girl?
Not made right, too large, needs to be thinner
Thinner
Thinner
Thinner
Snap.
Only 13, but you wish to be more.
More, give me more, I demand more.
Strive for perfection; you haven't reached it.

What are you doing, girl?
Limits you can never meet, you'd love to greet: 'Hello beauty.'
Whist the st-st-stutter of your voice box knocks over
to your depressing thoughts; it's all over.

You're too close to the light now; switch it off.
You're too close to the ceiling now; don't fall off.
Tie it tighter, tie it tighter, tie it tight.

No more.

Why did you do it, girl?
Pale skin, limp body.
You wish you were perfect.
But a girl can dream right?
You wished.

Tabitha Odutayo (14)
Harris Girls' Academy East Dulwich, London

I Am

I was a small girl
Lost and scared
All alone, no home
But now I'm found
Lifted from the ground

I am a big girl
Tall and strong
Being who I want to be
I'm going to be somebody
This is my life
I'll be free
I'll be who I want to be

Soon I'll be somebody
Known and found
I'll be a Ruler lifting people
From the ground
Rising them up
Making them free
Being who they want to be
All because of me

A small girl now big
Making a difference
Changing the world
The future
For the greater good

Jessica Mills (12)
Hayle Community School, Hayle

Dear Teachers

How well do you really see,
When you sit and look at me?
You may see a girl who struggles in class,
Finding it hard to solve her maths.
In geography, you see I cannot read maps well,
And in English you see me try hard to spell.
I'm the girl in the playground, hanging around,
Worrying about when that bell will sound.
You see a girl without an academic brain,
But every day I sit and play your game.

How well do you really see,
When you sit and look at me?
Well let me tell you who I really am,
When I'm not sat in school following your plan.
I'm the sparkly, bubbly girl, full of fun,
With determination and fire as bright as the sun.
I'm the girl, that will hold your hand when you cry,
The girl that never gives up and will forever try.
I'm a loving, loyal, caring friend,
Who will always offer my hand to lend.
All I really want is to make you all proud,
Just for once be me,
That stands out from the crowd.
So please, next time you look at me,
Look deep inside, see the real me.

Grace James (11)
Hayle Community School, Hayle

The Future

The future is a scary place
Moving from primary school to secondary
Moving from secondary to college
From college to a job.
But sometimes it can be some good.
Green grass slowly growing,
Wildlife expanding
From a village to a city.
This world is growing but it's also dying,
Buildings go up, trees go down.
The forests where animals are and live
Near the river drinking
As their homes get cut down.
They use wood for paper
In years ahead a new challenge is coming,
Many things are coming.
Oil will be gone,
Farms will be a city.
One day the world will be one city
As factories are made no land will be left,
The rivers will be in a large mess,
No green or much blue,
Hopefully we won't go too.
The population will grow,
People will die,
Materials will be gone for much but good,
Cars become hover cars,
Skateboards will be no fun.

Slowly this world is dying by the sun,
No trees, no us,
We float into space like a piece of dust.
Slowly we die, so make the most of it.
Slowly... we will disintegrate.

Sam Masters (12)
Hayle Community School, Hayle

Otto's Rainy Day

The trees blew softly in the silent rain and the gentle wind,
A few falling off because of the slight force of the wind
And hitting the wet stone floor.
He was watching this, watching this peaceful scenery,
The man had some messy braids, with flowers in-between the locks
Which were formed only a few minutes ago,
Now getting soaked by the calming rain.
His brown, large eyes reflected from the dim street lights,
Which were slowly turning on.
He didn't care if his dark freckled skin or furry coat got wet.
In fact, he slightly liked it -
The cold water cooling his hot and irritated skin.
The boy was so much in his 'fantasy world'
He could go to sleep.
On the elaborate metal bench
Under the large-leafed trees which protected him from the rain
And with the relaxing drops which hit the ground.
He thought to get up from the seat and go home
But trying to get up seemed too hard for him at the moment.
So, he laid on his head on the black painted metal
And thought to himself,
A small nap won't hurt you Otto...
And with those thoughts,
He closed his eyes...
And slept.

Julia Lutzka (12)
Hayle Community School, Hayle

Pheobe

She was dancing in red
Her name was Pheobe
She was the best dancer

I love her
She is beautiful and loving
The funniest person I know

Even though we can't be with each other
I still adore her
And so...
I asked her to dance

We danced in the night sky
With the moon's warm glow on us

So I say to her,
'I know we can't be together
But I will never stop loving you'

We spent our last magical night together
When we kissed the world stopped

We danced till the sun set

Ryan Harrison (12)
Hayle Community School, Hayle

My Life

It's amazing to be me,
I have cats and dogs next to me.
Cats are named Nana and Kitty,
Dogs, Rufus and Bruce.

An adorable little brother, Alex,
Who could resist - not me?
Amazing family and friends,
(Not for boys) but pink everything.
Pink bed, walls and carpet.

My mind is always sunny, no rain.
Everyone is good. Love is in the air.
But unfortunately not everyone can be like this.
Minds are not the same.

Jasmine Pearson (11)
Hayle Community School, Hayle

A World Without Humans

A world of humans being gone
Is a world of peace and song

Where the hills roll down and down
Where the mountains go up high upon a silver sky
Where the birds nest upon their nests
Where fish dart and dive
Where moles dig their holes
Where frogs jump and ribbit and croak
Where jaguars hiss and pounce
Where bees buzz and dance
Where life is great

Ben Pellow (12)
Hayle Community School, Hayle

Starlight

As the sun set
The stars rose
And twinkled through the night
As some headlights raced past the trees
From the road on the other side
Whilst the branches
From the huge dark tree
Stretched across the sky line
Waiting for you and me

Jowan Trewartha (12)
Hayle Community School, Hayle

The Beast Inside Me

The moon is like a lure, calling the wolf-like beast inside,
But for me, there's no place to hide,
As the light hits my eyes, the animal inside is calling.

Pain runs through me and I feel like I'm falling,
Everything hurts, my muscles, my bones,
But there is nothing I can do, when the beast inside me comes.

Though when I turn, no one understands,
I'm not a cold, bloodthirsty, heartless man,
I am an intelligent, reasonable person
But some disagree and a silver bullet will head my way and
Bang! goes the gun.

Hunters hate me, others don't really mind,
But no, you will butcher my kind,
I try to befriend you, I tell you, 'It will be fun,'
But when the beast inside me comes, and I tell you, 'Run!'
Just run!

Joanne Vallance (12)
John O'Gaunt School, Hungerford

The Life Cycle Of A Tree

Seed, deep in darkness,
Waiting patiently for growth,
Hidden from the world.

Seedling, just stolen,
Lifted away from the earth,
Taken far away.

New sapling shaking,
Surrounded by a clear cage,
Bent low by its weight.

Proud canopy spreads,
Growing,sheltering always,
Blossoming for joy.

Roots in the dry ground,
Branches sway gently, creaking,
Trunk stands stark and scarred.

Concrete wall looming
A stump, like graffiti, says:
'A NicE trEe woz 'Ere.'

Hannah Glover (14)
John O'Gaunt School, Hungerford

Climate Change

What type of world are you leaving for us?
Sensible, mature adults.
What type of world do you want us to inherit?
A broken one, obviously.

You claim you are tackling it,
Maybe you are?
All the debates, laws and equipment
Don't seem to be doing it,

It's still here.

What type of world are you leaving for us?
One polluted, the air is never clean.
What type of world do you want us to inherit?
A broken one, obviously.

Katherine Natton-Bell (12)
John O'Gaunt School, Hungerford

My Brain

My brain, a wonderful thing,
My brain, a triangle's ting,
My brain, anything but dumb,
My brain, the bash of a drum.

My brain contains many things,
But none of those things contain my brain.
The list goes on and on,
The list of my brain.

Emily Allsop (13)
John O'Gaunt School, Hungerford

When The Birds Stopped Singing

When the birds
stopped singing.
When the fortune cookies
gave bad fortune.
That's when I realised
that something was wrong.

I didn't know if it was
that war had started,
or that a life had come to an end.

I hastened to your place
because the trees told me something was wrong...

You didn't open
how you used to.

The only thing you said
was, 'Hello...'

And when I made jokes
you did not laugh

The doctor said nothing but
she must rest in peace -
Ever since I only saw you in the stars at night.

Rocio Lopez Lajo (12)
Reddam House, Wokingham

You And I

Remember that grand old oak tree that swayed in the breeze?
Remember that neat brown bench that sat beneath the trees?
Remember the sparrows and the birds that would sing flying by?
Remember when it was just, you and I?

That time we laughed together, swinging to and fro.
But now my life's not like that, I've hit the lowest of the low.
The dandelions in the field, and yes the roses too.
I remember all these times, now all I need is you.
I believed we could conquer the world together,
I believed we could even fly.
All that needs to be, is just you and I.

When we sat hand in hand, at the top of the hill.
When we strolled arm in arm, past the rusty mill.
When we laid down together, in the autumn leaves.
When all we wanted, was time just to freeze.
When we watched the lightning spark across the midnight sky.
We could be brighter than lightning, just you and I.

By the winter igloo and near the leafless trees.
By the park's rusty gates, no humming of the bees.
By the desolate town hall, no fire lit in there.
By the old park bench, wondering if this was really fair.
By the winter flowers, your chiselled, sweet stone grave.

By the beautiful frozen stream, thinking how much I crave
To spend one more day with you, would feel as if I could fly.

I'll repeat myself one more time, just for the comfort of you and I.

Remember that grand old oak tree that swayed in the breeze?
Remember that neat brown bench that sat beneath the trees?
Remember the sparrows and the birds that would sing flying by?
Remember when it was just,
You and I.

Max McLean (13)
Reddam House, Wokingham

A Paradise Reborn

The idyllic bubble of the country stream,
Glistening in the sunshine, so serene.
Slowly meandering down the gentle cascade,
Whilst its melodic tinkling continuously played.

Vast vibrant meadows of green,
Surrounding a kaleidoscopic sea of flowers, supreme
Majestic trees towering so high,
Their branches reaching up in an embrace with the sky.

The comforting hum of the breeze to be heard.
Its melody played by the chorus of birds.
Leaves tapping in a tranquil trance,
Whilst the tall swaying grass appears to dance.

You see, this future, a millennia away,
After self-gratifying man had caused decay...

They wiped themselves out with a nuclear war:
Subsequently the human race survives no more.

Yet Mother Nature has pulled through;
Now the Earth can start anew.

Jack Stannah (13)
Reddam House, Wokingham

Fairy

She came to me, she came to me,
Where I hid beneath the willow tree.
Blind eyes - but a heart that can see;
Oh I am fallen, falling in love.

She took my hand, she took my hand,
And pulled at me, guiding me to stand.
Beautiful wings - but grounded for me;
Oh I am fallen, falling in love.

She spread her wings, she spread her wings,
And treated me just as she would all kings.
Flying high - but holding on to me;
Oh I am fallen, falling in love.

Harriett Howard (12)
Reddam House, Wokingham

The Life Before

Full of nerves while thinking of you,
The new beginning rising,
Joyful when we're together,
Now my life ruined for the things you've done,
Sitting in my own little corner regretting my life,
Why is it so difficult to forget,
Close to me I feel relieved,
But when you get the knife out I get nervous or distressed,
Never knowing what you could be like.

Police, police I need your help. Help me, help me,
My devil is now locked forever,
Oh police, police you've pulled my life from the devil,
The devil of night.

I sit by a weeping willow,
Gazing into the sky,
Thinking of my freedom,
And my life gone by,
Wondering how I got through that,
The pain, nerves, exhaust,
No one wants to live like that,
Except for the people who can't get out,
No help, no money, no house, no life,
Never wanting my old life back,
A new start, a new beginning,
Doesn't everyone deserve a chance,
Make a wish, dream big, hope for the chance of freedom,
The life before is the life I don't want to go back to.

I put you in prison,
Where you belong,
The Devil in you is now locked forever,
Behind the stripes of rusty steel,
There's no hope of you getting out,
So good for you, think of the things you've done,
Regret every moment,
I'm never going back to the life I lived before,
My devil!

Natasha Blaize Archer (11)
Redroofs Theatre School, Maidenhead

The Last Time

(Lipogram - E)

I put my hand up high,
Stopping my body to cry,
Hoping contact will occur soon,
But for now my frustration is bursting as if it was a balloon,
As you and I float away in our own individual ways,
Thinking what a sunny day.

Lauren Murphy (12)
Redroofs Theatre School, Maidenhead

70

Lost In The Mountains

Lost,
Lost in the snow,
Lost where there is no hope.

Hoping,
Hoping to find shelter,
Hoping someone will help.

Help,
Help and find me,
Help or it will go wrong.

Wrong,
Wrong it was to come here,
Wrong would it be to not be in fear.

Fear,
Fear running through my veins,
Fear spreading through my freezing body.

Lost. No shelter. No help. Wrong turn. Fearing no return...

Katherine Bradshaw (11)
Ryde School With Upper Chine, Ryde

Growing Up

We get up, every day,
It's hard, but we do it anyway,
We go to school, we write stuff down,
Constantly receiving judgemental frowns.

We laugh and smile, we try to fit in,
But we know the truth behind the grins,
We're all scared, desperate to look good,
With our selfies on Instagram 'in the hood'.

Sometimes, we just want to stay home and sleep,
Some things we see online make us weep.
Your friends are partying, all night long,
And you're crying alone, thinking, *what did I do wrong?*

We feel more broken, angry and sad,
Not understanding why things turned out bad,
We want to look different, and be different too,
But we can't be bothered to even move.

So tell me, when did everything change?
When we didn't call anyone anything but by
their names?
When we didn't care about weight or height?
When none of us could read or write?

Maybe this is it, this is where it ends,
Childhood down the drain and losing all your 'friends'.
Growing up is hard, adolescence isn't fun,
Especially in a generation where girls your age,
Are becoming mums.

Aisling Nuttall (14)
Ryde School With Upper Chine, Ryde

Argument

Let the argument begin,
Hopefully, I will win.
'Mum, where shall I start?
I don't want to finish this chart.'

The maths is one big blur on the page,
The homework forms an unbreakable cage.
'But, Elsa this work is important you see.'
'Mum, I feel like I'd rather be up a tree.'

I stare past my monster mother,
Up the stairs, away from my brother,
But mum is there standing, a sentry at the door,
Therefore, I will have to declare war.

'Mum, I will not do any more subtraction,
I'm clearly having a negative reaction.'
With that, I stomped my foot
'Homework is worse than shovelling soot.'

Then I ran, up the stairs,
Past our red and black chairs.
Over the spotty, fluffy carpet.
Up and away from the homework tar pit!

From downstairs, I hear a roar.
Mum is acting like an enraged boar.
For in my plans there is one fatal flaw.
Mum's word is house law.

Elsa Wester (12)
Ryde School With Upper Chine, Ryde

Adulthood

You cannot see it,
You cannot stop it,
Yet it is still there,
Lingering in your hair.
In your eyes, your ears,
In your mouth and nose,
Still there.
Still holding you close.

To escape there is no hope,
No light.
For this foe you cannot fight.
It draws you nearer with every second,
It fascinates and it beacons.

A newborn baby's happy face,
Is not scarred with this disgrace.
No, no my friend, no indeed,
It preys on us and all children timid.
And we children are children no more,
But going into adulthood,
Bruised and sore.

Watch out!
Here it comes!
It's drawing close.
Take care you're in for a heavy dose!
But for all its anger,
And vicious snappiness,
It brings love, joy,
And maybe, just maybe,
Happiness...

Sneha Sanyal (12)
Ryde School With Upper Chine, Ryde

All Over Time

Towers fall and bridges collapse,
Planes fly and trains ride,
New buildings are built,
Whilst others will wilt,
As they get knocked down in time.

The life on other planets
Will come to the world.
The planet will heat up,
And the sun will grow,
Scorching the Earth's round face,
The ice caps will melt and rivers will flow,
To inspissate the universe pace,
As the world spins in time.

The oceans will dry out,
And creatures will become extinct,
Desert sands will blow about,
Lightly in the wind.
Cities in the south will become abandoned
Whilst others in the north will become
More popular all over time.

Now the skies are our paths,
The fields are our road
The rivers are our seas,
The rainforests are dry
Vegetation dies out and plains occur,
This is what happens all over time.

Tilly Ashton (12)
Ryde School With Upper Chine, Ryde

Hopes And Fears

Hopes and fears, we all have them,
Sometimes we let them show.
They are all individual,
No matter where we go.

What are your fears?
What makes you scared.
What makes you hide in the corner?
Has anyone even cared?

What is your biggest dream?
It can be anything you choose,
It could be to win a race,
But what would happen if you lose?

But if you were to win the race,
What would your reaction be?
Could it be, you shout hip hip hooray
Or go out for some posh tea?

You might want to be a doctor,
Saving lots of lives.
Spiders could be your worst fear,
With all their little eyes.

Hopes and fears, we all have them,
Sometimes we let them show.
They are all individual,
No matter where we go.

Florence Tweddle (12)
Ryde School With Upper Chine, Ryde

A Dystopian Tale

My shattered face, squinted at the murky skies,
Black circling high
Like a lost fly, about to fall.

Red and black callings entered my ears,
Despair, tragedy, I could hear
Piercing like a spear, about to fall.

From the bitter ground to the ripped up clouds,
Battle cries, blood streaming loud
Pain rushing, round and around about to fall.

The battered soldiers, treading down war.
Mankind's opponent, deadly as a chainsaw.
Extinction, scraping the floor about to fall.

When my muscles gave out, no rest, no noon,
Harsh metal, throughout sun and moon
An overdosed spoon, about to fall.

Fear smacked me, so hard as the nightmoss ran
The lights went out, the only man.
But then a punch, deep low
The 'on' button, head to toe.
This part of me, would not fall.

Ben Haworth (12)
Ryde School With Upper Chine, Ryde

What Does The Future Hold?

Technology's future, a haunting trap so hard to escape,
A burgen-like weight,
You can't let go
However avoidance is no option.
The daggers of grey citizens inspissate,
Killing the aspect of time.
Conference meetings oil the cogs of the production line.

Click! Another iPhone is ready.
Seeking a child to go and steal their proper life,
Forcing their thumbs to keep tapping.

A shopkeeper braces himself for the accumulating crowds,
Bound to the new product as it is placed on the shelf.

Apple and Samsung draw the equation,
1 year = 5 or more products.

Social media, like a virus, attacking whoever it can.
A haunting trap so hard to escape,
Will you submit?

Jacob Swann (12)
Ryde School With Upper Chine, Ryde

D.T.

Sawing, bending, welding, sanding,
Mr Hoare is never a bore,
You can't get his head under the door,
Because he's so tall he makes me feel small
He's the best at D.T.

The screeching of the angle grinder,
Seems to make him kinder,
He's never in a grumpy mood,
Even if I've just glued the floor.

If you need some help he'll never yelp,
He'll be there in a flash,
I'm making a Go-Kart
It's lots more fun than art, drawing pointless things.

The blinding blue sparks that never make marks,
Are as cool as can be.
The sander roars like a lion,
I'm surprised he never wants a lie in!

Alex Wilson (12)
Ryde School With Upper Chine, Ryde

Somewhere I Like To Go

In the winter silent and bare,
In the summer we play truth or dare.
The sun is a smiling face,
I wish to be nowhere but this place.

The sea is a roaring bear,
And wind blows through my hair.
The stones are sparkling eyes.
In the evening there are a million skies.

The sun is red with anger.
And the boats race until there is a winner!
We love the picnics on the beach,
Sausages are our favourite to eat!

In the evening the sun falls from the sky,
And the moon rises like a snow white eye.
The children go in,
And the lights turn on,
The moon seems to say goodnight everyone!

Ella Morgan Laird (12)
Ryde School With Upper Chine, Ryde

Freshwater Bay

Like a sapphire sparkling,
The jewel of the bay
Calls with the sound of its waves,
For you to stay.

Towering above, crumbling castle walls,
Bright chalky white,
Hold you captive in wonder,
As seagulls take flight.

Kayaks gliding across the surface,
Surfers rolling with the waves,
Children inspecting the rock pools,
Exploring the deep, dark caves.

At the end of the day,
Say goodbye to the sun,
Memories of laughter-filled adventure
And buckets of fun.

Edward Ardley (12)
Ryde School With Upper Chine, Ryde

Memories

As I look back into the past
I'm filled with memories, that are vast,
As I look deeper, I see joy and fun,
And I wish that nothing was done.

As I stay here in the present,
I learn more and more new lessons;
I see the friendships I have made
Like they would never fade.

As I look to the future,
I picture moments of sadness;
But they never last
For I have friends, family and love.

Daisy Pink (11)
Ryde School With Upper Chine, Ryde

Silenced Souls

T, t t t, t t, t t t.
Ting!
A room in silence,
Unaware of what conversation brings.

Desperate people on black and white screens,
Too scared to discover the natural landscape.
It's like the phone has actually possessed them,
As if the phone is their only escape.

Lonely people in a darkened room,
Oblivious to the master's patrols,
Living their lives as
Silenced souls.

Thomas Luke (12)
Ryde School With Upper Chine, Ryde

The Day The 'Others' Took Over Planet Blue

(Written in the dystopian future of May 1st 3576)

At this height he feels amazed,
The dark tempting azure as far as gaze.
Happy souls have found a place to rest
One of the places he knows best.

Large chalk walks tower the wrinkled sea,
The sun, a soul reaching out as far as can be,
His family's souls still have nothing to see.

The shattered mirror reflects our souls,
God has emptied our once joyful bowls,
We have come to an agreement of the past,
An agreement that will surely last.

Imran Rahman (11)
Ryde School With Upper Chine, Ryde

Hope Beach

The beach is a gold mine,
The sand is the precious gold,
The waves that crash against the shore,
Is the cave protecting the glistening gold,
The laughter heard upon the beach,
Is the joy when gold miners find the gold.
The glorious, summer sun that beats down every day,
Is that stunning piece of gold that everyone desires,
The hope from the name,
Is the hope goldseekers hold,
The beach is a gold mine,
It spreads the happiness everyone craves.

Caitlin Dingle (12)
Ryde School With Upper Chine, Ryde

Global War

I sit on my couch enjoying my tea
I watch the telly

But in other places around the world
People are screaming
Hiding from the dangers that surround them at all times
I hear on the news
People are dying because of these terrible wars

Hearing about the mess that war can do
Makes tears flood out of my eyes into a puddle that never absorbs

All around the world
You hear and see people pleading for money
Fleeing to safety
Sending mothers and their children away
Whilst fathers stay behind and fight for their countries

I feel guilt I'm in a house where it's safe
Sometimes the most unfortunate things happen
We have Big Brother watching over us

When I'm sitting there
Just listening
It breaks my heart

All I wanna do is jump up and help
Try to settle the ground
I can't do it on my own

So our country helps
They send army troops out
And become allies

Slowly things change
Some areas of the globe
Wave a white flag but others carry on
To show they can't be beaten

Shravani Philpot (14)
Simmons House Classroom, London

Isolation

Isolation,
Hey look, there she is all alone
With no friends.
Not even a leaf will go near her.
Alone she sits.
Alone she stays.
She sits on her very own table
Not because she's greedy or fat,
But because nobody likes her.
Friend is just a word
That means happiness to her
The total opposite of her constant emotion
Isolation is,
Her only reason to live.

Jade Ball (11)
St Leonards Academy, St Leonards-On-Sea

The Nightmare!

A stormy night,
Trees dance wildly,
The boy sleeping awakes,
The shadow of the tree,
Flies by the window,
'Argh a monster,'
Screams in fear,
The moon rises higher,
Revealing the monster as a tree,
He falls backwards into his bed,
Lightning strikes the tree,
Iridescently the tree glows green,
Fire approaches,

Sun rising,
Rain falling,
The fire slowly,
Dies out,
The boy is safe now,
No more nightmares...

Millie Kemp (12)
St Leonards Academy, St Leonards-On-Sea

Tears

Please forgive me,
For I now know what not to do,
The truth is that I'm lying.

I put my heart on the line,
But you hung up.

You say there is light,
But all I see is the night.

On my cheek,
By your graveside,
One drop, one drop that meant a lot.

Now I lay me down to sleep,
A leaden heart is mine to keep.
If I should die before I wake,
Now there's an offer I'd gladly take.

Too tired to fight,
Can't cope, can't cope,
No way to regain my repossessed hope.

Every time I think of you,
I shed more than a tear or two.

Why did we have to depart,
When we were bound at heart.

Love for me, was never a game,
And I still love you the very same.

My silence is just another word for my pain,
And this is a lonely year again and again.

Death is not the end,
But the start of a new life.

Lucy Green (13)
St Leonards Academy, St Leonards-On-Sea

Death

I wake up tomorrow
To find you're not there
But you are up there
In the best of care
It will cause you pain
And you will not gain
For the rain that's on your grave
At a flick of a finger
At the pull of a trigger
Someone dies each second
But you will remember
The pillows of the sky
Will hold your soul and mine
When my time is up
I will rise above
So never say goodbye
So they are never gone
So death cannot do wrong

Adam Elfero (12)
St Leonards Academy, St Leonards-On-Sea

The Art Of Teaching Karate

Watching the years fade by,
As I see the colours go by.
Working my hardest so they feel good,
Travelling through my childhood.

I give out punches and kicks,
As I speak through the tricks.
Constantly correcting,
Constantly awarding.

I teach them a sequence of moves,
For them to say, 'What do I do?'
It's OK as I clamp my hooves,
But re-teach them what to do.

Lewis Greathead (13)
St Leonards Academy, St Leonards-On-Sea

Bullying

Bullying, who needs it
It hurts, it isolates and it kills
Why, a lot of people ask
Why do they do it?
The don't understand
They don't know what they are doing to their victim.
They want a reaction they know where to go for that
They know what buttons to push
We *must* stop it
We must
Bullying hurts, isolates and kills
Think
Stop.

Chelsey Kelly (13)
St Leonards Academy, St Leonards-On-Sea

Have You Ever Wondered?

Have you ever wondered if it was possible to freeze time?
Have you ever wondered what it would be like if you could travel through time?
Have you ever wondered what it would be like if you could change how the world works?
But what if it all came true?
Could you make the world a better place?
Could you change what happened in the past?
Could you freeze time?
Could you prevent wars from happening
Have you ever? Have you ever?

Shakira Helsdown (14)
St Leonards Academy, St Leonards-On-Sea

The Lake Glider

She glides, she's shy, and she knows she can be seen
She knows she is a target she cruises around the lake like a
Luxury Maybach, but her bodyguards can't be seen...
She's like a high class celebrity of the lake
But she has to be careful of the lip piercing
She can't even feed without being careful - she knows
The angler wants her. She knows her bodyguards can't
Be seen, so when she gets a lip piercing she won't
Go down without a fight - like a boxer fighting for her title
She's the lake champion for two seasons, but she slips up
And loses to the carp killer.

Sam Hinton
The Gryphon School, Sherborne

The Judgement

How is it that 12 people can decide,
When nine kids don't understand death nor life?
All of the pain when they lay their head
It doesn't hurt anymore when they go to bed

You may be free in the eyes of the law
But these streets you will walk no more
The way you treated us - it was dirty
So you and your man could be flirty

Nine children: you lost us all
Don't think you'll ever get us back - you fool!
Words came out, so many unheard,
Yet you walk around as if you are as free as a bird

Our family destroyed, no place of stability
You're a mum again now, but there is no opportunity,
You never bothered and I lost every hope,
Now you just sit in the dock and mope

One day, I assure you, we will meet again
Whether in sunshine or in rain
My trust in you, you will never get
I'll do myself proud, because you I'll forget.

M (16)
The Hope Service, Guildford

Her

Her eyes
Her eyes are trees out of her face,
Staring at you as you walk by

Her hair
Her hair is sharp metal wire
Scratching wherever you go

Her teeth
Black knives un-arranged in her mouth
When she bites you, you bleed to death

Her cheeks
They are as red as the Red Sea
Drowning you wildly

Her nose
As big as a shark in a pond
Exploding with blood

But her house,
Her family buried in the garden,
The stench is unbearable
Caped in fog and brambles

She just sits,
No expression
Black clothing

The worst thing is
If you enter
You won't come out alive.

Maisie Craven-Smith (13)
Warminster School, Warminster

The Girl

She stood there,
Eyes searching.
But who knows why?
Then they fell upon me.

I felt them boring into me,
Like daggers slitting my skin.
As she came towards me,
I felt shivers in my spine.

She held me down with her glare
As I heard her roar,
'Who goes there?'
Then the corners of my vision went dark.

A few seconds later,
The world went black
And I felt cold, ghostly arms
Ease me onto my side

As I fell into a gentle slumber.
I heard air whizzing past
As if I was in a plane
With the doors and windows open.

I came to a sudden halt
Dreading what I was to see:
I saw myself in a dark room,
With a girl in a white dress, staring at me.

Rose Elsden (13)
Warminster School, Warminster

The Nightmare

Asleep, your twisted mind is released
Asleep, you can forget who you are meant to be
Asleep, all your infinite troubles fade into darkness
Asleep, the monstrous nightmares are set free.

Fear, your heart stops beating
Fear, the unmerciful laughter echoes through your ears
Fear, the blood-curdling monster's shadows draw you in
Fear, fight the tears

Pain, slithers up your warped spine
Pain, spreads like an allergic reaction, unable to control
Pain, beats you up and knocks you down
Pain, caresses your soul

Awake, the nightmare's creep back into the unlit corners of your brain
Awake, the nightmare is merely a memory
Awake, you take over the terror
Awake, that is the beauty of a nightmare you see.

Milly Morgan (12)
Warminster School, Warminster

The Spidery Tree

I sat beneath a spidery tree
Its broken legs all around me
The watery sun made lace on the ground
And bathed the dying leaves all around.

I felt so sad as I thought of my life
Dwindling and trickling, I took out my knife
And watched it smiling, glinting at me
Beneath the spidery tree.

The leaves stirred round as the wind blew strong
Lifting higher my thoughts; I could be wrong
I shivered and looked to the comforting roots
And saw a tiny flower crushed beneath my boots.

Get from me, knife I said, and take
Your gleaming cruel blade, I'll make
A use for you away from death
And life shall come back from underneath.

James Burn-Leefe (13)
Warminster School, Warminster

The House On The Moors

The house on the moors,
Deep in Yorkshire you will find it,
At full moon and twelfth strike,
Then the scares happen.
The sound of crushing rock,
Gargoyles start to awaken,
After one month stuck in their position,
Sighing before but now they start to cry.
The smell of bitter blood haunts the hall,
Meaning the bats have turned to their normal form,
The clicking of boots coming down the stairs,
Faces start to appear with crimson liquid on their sinful grins.
Creature after creature,
Arriving like an army,
Goblins behind witches,
Zombies following ghosts
All there to plan the approach of the century.
That's what goes on at the house on the moors.

Lucy Farey (13)
Warminster School, Warminster

The Room

Imagine a room filled with all of your fears
That makes you weep nothing more than tears.
You try to tell yourself to settle down.
But in the corner of the room your eyes meet with a clown
It grins then turns to the figure chuckling in the dark
But then you hear the calling of a lark
You sit up and think it was all a dream
But then you hear an ear-piercing scream
You look around and you're back in the room.
And a match strikes, dispelling the gloom

A scythe reflects the burning flame
'Reveal your name or your life I'll claim!'
You stand there, hopeless, saying nothing
You hear the figure that watches still chuckling
Death drags you down to your certain doom
You wish you could leave the dreadful room.

Archie Fogg (13)
Warminster School, Warminster

The Journey

The rhythmic thud of the train is all I can hear
In the cramped cattle carriage,
I can still smell the cows that once stood in this obsolete wagon.
The swaying should be soothing but we all stand in rigid silence;
We grind to a halt and an immense fear rises in the pit of my stomach
Fear is now all you can smell.
In my seven years of life I have never experienced anything
as horrible as this;
The door opens, in rushes the freezing air,
It hits me like a punch to the guts.
We are dragged out like cattle and herded down a track.
How can so many people make such little noise?
I look up and see the wire fence scaling up like a sheer cliff face,
There in front of me are rows of ghost like faces with empty eyes.
We all know our terrible fate at Auschwitz but say nothing,
This was my one and only train journey.

Ronan McKeigue (12)
Warminster School, Warminster

Through The Woods

Stealing, secretly, silently through the mist,
My eyes with slumber kissed,
The trees so tight with a sacred bond,
Into the unknown beyond,
Lost and found,
My heart is bound,
And onwards into the gloom,
Towards my almost certain tomb,

Stealing, secretly, silently through the trees,
I feel so strangled with unease,
Closer, closer still,
My legs walking against my will,
The guilt, the untouchable remorse,
Weighing me down like a cart horse.
Whatever spurred me on I'll never know,
I feel as if the time I'm using is borrowed.

Stealing, secretly, silently to my inevitable grave,
For once I know I must be brave.

Thea Knight (13)
Warminster School, Warminster

Life At The Park

It was all going great, great at the park
We were all having fun just having a laugh
My mind turned dark like a deep dark cave,
My head was reckless,
Like a daze.

I was down on my knees, begging please,
Hoping adventurous thoughts would come to me,
Please Mr Bully, I don't know what to do,
My poor life can't explain what I did to you.
You take all my stuff,
You search all my bags,
Your features are so horrible
You're really bad.

So now I'm back at the park all alone,
Now you've got your royalty
You've got your throne.

Jade Louise Baldwin (13)
Wilmington Academy, Dartford

Emotions - What Could They Be?

Hearing the alarm ring
Getting ready for the day
Throwing my tears away
Living with three boys - wow! What a noise!
Seeing my friends is the best part of the day
Making sure I am okay
Back home again
Having food
Oh gosh! What to do?
Ringing my mum
Making sure I'm having fun
Maybe ringing some friends
Nobody knows how this could end
The gossip and chit-chat
The banter untold
Making sure our friendship can hold
Everything, everyone, how chaotic
Making sure my life's exotic
These are my emotions
What are yours?
Lights off, all quiet
So peaceful,
Goodbye!

Millie Edmundson (12)
Wilmington Academy, Dartford

The Future Is Untold

The future what will it hold?
A creature of untold.
The iPhone 25, what will it be,
A guardian, that's what it could be.

What about the cars, will they fly?
Maybe land in outer sky.
Nobody knows,
Maybe God cares,
But maybe I do,
Then the future is there.

Jetpacks, how fun that would be,
Flying to school, that would be great.
School maybe a new theme,
Books no more, tech is here.
The imagination grows wild,
Who knows what's untold.
TV, what will happen to that,
Maybe a new model or theme.
The TV could come to life,
The story would thrive.

Sport, will it be here?
Maybe a new era will appear.
Maybe flying hockey,
The tension high,
Footballers won what a blast,
There will be a big past

The future is there to be held,
Embrace and enjoy, whatever will be told.

Bradley Alan Sapsford (12)
Wilmington Academy, Dartford

Teenager

You have to be skinny,
Have hair to the floor
Get 100 likes,
Or just don't bother at all.

Have you got an iPhone?
What about Snapchat?
How may boys are you talking to,
How many adore?

You've got no friends,
You're a lesbian too,
Don't join a club,
You can't be different too.
Only laugh at my jokes,
Don't have your hair short.

You can't wear that,
You look ugly and all,
It's not easy being a teenager.

Grace Nash
Wilmington Academy, Dartford

About The Boy

Like a moody mare,
She started to stare at boys,
She wanted to talk to him,
But she was too scared.

She turned around and he was there,
But not for long
Then he was gone,
And he was right behind her.

She was scared
But he was there,
She said to herself,
Say something, say something.

She froze
Humiliated herself,
That was the end,
Of the boy she loved.

Madison Stockburn
Wilmington Academy, Dartford

Stress Of Life!

What is happening?
What do I do?
I'm getting stressed out,
Please help!

The stress is taking over,
It's like a bullet through my brain.
My emotions are going up and down,
It's like a roller coaster.

The wind is howling with its rage,
Louder and louder it's growing,
Fences are smashing,
Cats are screeching,
Silence...
Not a sound in the sky,
It has stopped now.

Dylan Carter Booth (13)
Wilmington Academy, Dartford

The Future

What will our future hold?
Will it be hot or cold?
Self-driving cars
Creatures in the ground
Will there be people living on Mars?
Will there be treasure to be found?
Infinite money
The world would be funny
What will our future hold?

Bang! Flash!
No more cash
Everything is gone
The world has gone wrong
What will our future hold?

Finlay Goodger (12)
Wilmington Academy, Dartford

The Chimp

Victims act like happy chimps,
Then along comes the brutal hunters,
The monkey's soul dissolves
The hunter shoots
The monkey crumbles
Volcanoes erupt from the chimp's eyes
The hunters laugh.
The monkey evolves into a destructive gorilla
The hunter comes back and makes the gorilla.
The gorilla laughs and charges with desire.
The hunter runs and corners.
The hunter shoots another chimp.
The gorilla charges and shoots the shooter.
The hunter cries in pain and agony.
The gorilla takes the monkey under his wing.
The hunter runs and never shoots again.

Ben Gifford (12)
Wilmington Academy, Dartford

The End

The buildings tumble,
Whilst the ground crumbles,
It is everywhere.
Dead bodies right there,
The whole world has gone mad,
Whilst the rich people are glad.

The ocean is full of oil,
However you can't see any soil
Everybody wears animal skins,
I just hope this will end.

The whole world is orange,
With all the fire roaring,
Soon the world will end.

Sonny George Anderson (13)
Wilmington Academy, Dartford

The Fashion World

A hurricane of clothes fills the table,
Mannequins pose for the camera,
Lights flashing in their eyes,
Red carpet covers the ground,
And this was the fashion world,
That I lived in.

The air was filled with the most wonderful smell,
Music played as they walked the red carpet,
Worrying about how to cut the right size,
Making sure the clothes match,
So many things need to go right,
Just one more night,
Then it will be alright.

Kennedy Bates (12)
Wilmington Academy, Dartford

Favourite Class

There is a cloud over my head,
Making me gloomy and sad.
The sun shines through as
I walked to my favourite class.
I start to become myself,
I let all my worries go.
My mind, my body are no longer
Controlled. I am free!
As it ends.
I'm controlled again.
I have to go back to reality.
Reality is a tragedy.
I'll have to wait...

Millie Rose (13)
Wilmington Academy, Dartford

Untitled

That day they forgot,
That day that I dread,
It was that day I was going to get shot,
The bullet would have gone right through my head.
It was like a nightmare,
But a million times worse,
When will they learn to treat people fair?
It was that day they ripped my shirt.
They took all my money
Left me in pain
They thought it was funny,
Left the blood to spill and stain.

Archie Copley (11)
Wilmington Academy, Dartford

Emotions

I'm happy now,
So it needs to stay that way.
No more fights, and no more arguing
So that's the way it needs to be.
I have finally got across the tightrope.

I'm sad now
So I need to change,
I found it hard to stay good for awhile,
So I need to change,
I have fallen off the tightrope for being bad.

George Warner (12)
Wilmington Academy, Dartford

Confusion

The world is changing for the greater good,
Technology is improving,
And humans are not!
They're taking over,
They're taking our jobs,
And leaving us with nothing,
This is unacceptable,
We're like sitting ducks,
Waiting for the inevitable to happen,
They're everywhere I go,
I feel like I'm being stalked.

Louis James Childs (13)
Wilmington Academy, Dartford

Emotions

One minute, I'm happy,
Then I'm not!
My emotions are getting me down.
I'm just someone, I'm not!
What's wrong with me?
Why am I like this?
Will I ever know?
My mum screams!
My dad shouts!
I can't take this!
What do I do?

Floss Goulter (12)
Wilmington Academy, Dartford

What The Future Holds?

The young boy stood, trembling like a cub that's lost his mother.
The green wasteland surrounded him.
What once was a city with people rushing around,
Minding their own business, is now old, run down skyscrapers,
So old that they lean on each other for support.
Green weeds with thick branches dominated the skyscrapers
Causing them to topple like Jenga.
Smoke filled the land,
Bodies of the deceased lay strewn like unwanted toys.
All that remained was silence.

Jaden Rose
Wilmington Academy, Dartford

Confusion

Confusion is one of my fears,
It might consume me,
Though it is rare,
It brings control,

Comes and goes as it please,
My lucid dreams vanished,
Lets my demons at ease,
It brings darkness

Bad actions I've accepted,
Though I never forgot,
All my desires rested,
But I fought hard,

My confusion grows and grows,
Like a fire inside me,
Wish I could tie it with a bow,
And send it away for eternity,

Knowledge is a powerful weapon,
One I don't hold,
My key will come,
As the door stays closed,

But I've fought hard and stayed strong,
My fear keeps me alive,
That's my greatest bond,
A bond connected to my mind,

Confusion is one my fear,
Though I start to understand,
Things that stay unclear,
Just needs a little hand,

It brings regret and control,
It also brings determination,
To find answers and all,
To find motivation.

Shannon Enishta Mattarooa (14)
Winchmore School, London

Vitamin Intelligence

Books, books
How wonderful they are
Books are the real gems
Worth more than any diamond

I've been around the world
Visited extraordinary kingdoms
Sailed the seven seas
Met my best friends, foes and forever homes
Every time I hear the beautiful sound of the flapping of pages
Swish! Swish! Flick!
I'm lost in a sea of endless sentences
What storms shook the boat my dreams are in
Luckily my passport has never ending pages!

I have a taste for the fruit of knowledge
So the library is where I am buried in for hours
Books are the seeds that plants my wisdom
My imagination is the oxygen and water that nourishes the plant
Let your eyes drink up the words
'Oh wonderful book, don't you ever run out of sacred pleasure?'
Books give laughter, books give sorrow
Laughter is the music of the soul; before I know it,
my heart is a sea of tears
When in the mines of engineered words, similes, metaphors
and thoughts
I take a cart to discover the wonders that await me

My heart blazes every time I sink into the yellow pages since the yellow
pages are my sunlight
Giving me 'vitamin intelligence' every time I am exposed to it and every
time I'm exposed to vitamin intelligence,
My mind is closer to be equal to a computer

And when we come to the end of our adventure,
Just as a wise person once said:
'Don't cry because it ended. Smile because it happened.'
After that, we could go to the library and borrow another adventure.

Aleyna Degirmen (12)
Winchmore School, London

War Of The Tattooed Summoner

On my hand is the pentacle tattooed,
By my side stands Ignite,
My wolfish companion in all his might,
To the Orcs, to the enslavement of the Myths, my battle is set,
They shall be freed,
By me and my Wogeran, you'll all see.

On a mission of stealth, to infiltrate all infidel,
Ignite roars for his wolfish blood to be returned to the Ether World,
The Orcs make the myths slave away,
Draining their mana... day by day...

I infuse Ignite to sharpen my senses,
I will summon him when we access to their defences,
Myths will put aside our differences,
To beat a common enemy,
We will take down the Orcs' 'invincible' army,
So hear my cry of 'Freedom's Revolution,'
And let their bodies succumb to my potions!

At last the battle is through,
But also comes the most dangerous journey too
They say to be a true master you must be brave,
However a true master must be not,
As the Ether World is the most dangerous place,
Where mutated eagles will attack anything near their space
But fast and true do I realise that Ignite is by my side,
And together, we know as one, that we shall win the battle that is soon
to come.

The punishments of 'desertion' are extremely vile,
Although I don't fear exile,
I fear my family will face the people of scepticism,
And all of the useless excuses Government will throw,
I don't want to go back to my home...

Mustafa-Berk Ak (12)
Winchmore School, London

Alone

I'm isolated,
I'm miserable.
Although my leaves are as bright as the sun,
They might as well be black,
The colour of death.
Swish!
I feel naked as my leaves swiftly plunge to the ground,
Nowadays all I hear is that dreadful sound.
Winter is coming at the blink of an eye,
It's just so near,
It's definitely the most depressing time of the year.
I care about you a lot.
Why don't you care about me?
Every day I provide you with oxygen to breathe,
And how do you repay me?
You cause havoc and chaos,
Then you cut down my family.
I've lived for generations,
I've seen your grandparents and your great ones too,
They never did what you're doing to me.
What happened to society?
Remember this,
One day when I'm long gone,
You will understand the mistakes you're making.
Hopefully you will realise what you're doing and the risk you're taking.
When that day comes, I pray that it's not too late.

Klea Ndoj (12)
Winchmore School, London

In Memorium

(This poem is dedicated to Matthew Brittan, a brilliant friend and incredible person who was there for me when I needed a friend, who tragically took his own life 1st Feb 2016, 14 years old.)

Goodbye, see you tomorrow
Same as every day except
Not the same.
In your vision, I never saw the sorrow
Never saw the pain in your eyes
Light the way forward, through the darkest tunnel.
All us with you, all agree
A good friend in you, the best,
The brightest, the most approachable
A good friend indeed.
Face is apparent, anywhere you'd be,
You were seen, a beacon
A hope to the hopeless.
To guide us all from crashing waves,
Shattered rocks, to the safety of shore.
The guard house, the keep to keep,
Spirit of happiness, and joy,
Though suffering played, none reached us.
Through you walked alone, we all walked with you.
Evil, cruellest, fateful twist.
Unfair, to he who would stand against highest odds... By your side.
Wish there was a way to repay the favour.
My friend, he whose smile would light the room,
He who kept dark inside, so we wouldn't see,
He who died too young.
Why? I ask.
Why? I cry.
Why didn't you tell us, so we could save you?
Why? mutters the winds.

Why did you feel such pain?
We could have helped you, but we didn't know.
Did you ask yourself if you could tell us of your pains and fears?
Did you feel alone?
Did you feel anger towards us or yourself?
Let your soul rest forever, away from prying eyes, where sadness cries,
But go to a place where the sun doesn't die,
where no one cries and no one dies.
To a place where you can leave the armour of image behind,
Lower the walls of your mind,
Drop the world, to be free.
Leave the demons behind, the demons with
Blood-red eyes.
Take yourself beyond, to silver,
scarlet, sunburst skies.
To a place where there is piece of mind, where no one cries,
And no one dies.
To a place where you'll be recognised, for the noble,
Caring, brilliant person you were
Get away from the electric eye of the false images,
Get away from the pressure of expectations,
But remember us, wherever you go,
Because we will remember you,
My dearest friend.

Leon Malins (14)
Worle Community School, Weston-Super-Mare

YoungWriters

Est. 1991

YOUNG WRITERS INFORMATION

We hope you have enjoyed reading this book – and that you will continue to in the coming years.

If you're a young writer who enjoys reading and creative writing, or the parent of an enthusiastic poet or story writer, do visit our website www.youngwriters.co.uk. Here you will find free competitions, workshops and games, as well as recommended reads, a poetry glossary and our blog.

If you would like to order further copies of this book, or any of our other titles give us a call or visit **www.youngwriters.co.uk**.

Young Writers
Remus House
Coltsfoot Drive
Peterborough
PE2 9BF

(01733) 890066
info@youngwriters.co.uk